I0079275

Proverbs:
Pathways to Wisdom

Leader Guide

Proverbs: Pathways to Wisdom

Proverbs
   978-1-5018-9429-9
   978-1-5018-9430-5 eBook

Proverbs DVD
   978-1-5018-9433-6

Proverbs: Leader Guide
   978-1-5018-9431-2
   978-1-5018-9432-9 eBook

DOMINICK S. HERNÁNDEZ

PROVERBS

PATHWAYS TO WISDOM

LEADER GUIDE

BY KEVIN C. NEECE

Abingdon Press / Nashville

Proverbs: Pathways to Wisdom
Leader Guide

Copyright © 2020 Abingdon Press
All rights reserved.

No part of this work may be reproduced or transmitted in any form or by any means, electronic or mechanical, including photocopying and recording, or by any information storage or retrieval system, except as may be expressly permitted by the 1976 Copyright Act or in writing from the publisher. Requests for permission can be addressed to Permissions, The United Methodist Publishing House, 2222 Rosa L. Parks Blvd., Nashville, TN 37228-1306 or emailed to permissions@umpublishing.org.

978-1-5018-9431-2

Unless otherwise indicated, all Scripture quotations are from the ESV® Bible (The Holy Bible, English Standard Version®), copyright © 2001 by Crossway, a publishing ministry of Good News Publishers. Used by permission. All rights reserved.

20 21 22 23 24 25 26 27 28 29 — 10 9 8 7 6 5 4 3 2 1
MANUFACTURED IN THE UNITED STATES OF AMERICA

Contents

To the Leader

Wisdom is a pathway. As the leader of this study, you will serve as both guide and fellow traveler with others on this pathway. You will be aided in this journey both by a knowledgeable biblical scholar and by this Leader Guide, taking you and your fellow travelers, step by step, to a greater understanding of Proverbs, Scripture, and wisdom itself.

This Leader Guide is designed to be used with Dominick S. Hernández's book, *Proverbs: Pathways to Wisdom*. Dr. Hernández is an assistant professor of Old Testament Interpretation and the Director of the Online Hispanic Program at The Southern Baptist Theological Seminary in Louisville, Kentucky. As he continues to research, present, and write within academia, Dr. Hernández also gives seminars in the areas of Second Temple period Judaism, Old Testament, and Jewish holidays. He was trained in Semitic Philology at Bar-Ilan University in Ramat Gan, Israel, where he also earned his PhD in Hebrew Bible. Having served as an assistant professor of Bible for two years at Moody Bible Institute, Dr. Hernández now teaches on Near Eastern Literature, the Dead Sea Scrolls, and biblical wisdom literature, including the Book of Proverbs.

Dr. Hernández brings all of this expertise with him as he examines the Book of Proverbs and suggests not only a lens through which to view its wise sayings but also a method of approach that will help illuminate their meaning. Dividing his approach into four major elements, he explores pathways for understanding—pathways to wisdom—as well as ways to apply the wisdom of the proverbs in everyday life. Readers will find Dr. Hernández an able and engaging guide along these wisdom pathways and find themselves refreshed and encouraged along the way.

This Leader Guide provides you with the resources you need to lead a group through this study. It's likely that you will have more than enough material. So, you can choose from the options in the "Learning Together" sections to fit the time you have for your group meetings.

There are four sessions in this study, and they make use of the following components:

- Dr. Dominick S. Hernández's book titled *Proverbs: Pathways to Wisdom*
- The *Proverbs: Pathways to Wisdom* DVD (Or if you prefer, you may purchase streaming video files at www.Cokesbury.com. Or you may access the videos for this study on Amplifymedia.com through an individual or church membership.)
- This Leader Guide

Participants in the study should plan on bringing Bibles and a copy of *Proverbs: Pathways to Wisdom* to each session. If possible, notify those interested in the study in advance of the first session. Make arrangements for them to get copies of the book so they can read the introduction and chapter 1 before the first group meeting.

USING THIS GUIDE WITH YOUR GROUP

What will you find in this guide? A session format is below. It is designed to give you options and flexibility in planning your sessions with your group. You will want to develop your sessions with your group in mind, because different groups will have different interests as well as different dynamics. Choose any or all of the activities. Adapt. Reorder. Rearrange. Innovate. Here you will find the raw material for your lesson planning.

The session plans in this Leader Guide are designed to be completed in about 60 to 90 minutes, but you can use fewer activities to reduce the time to as little as 45 minutes. Depending on which activities you select, there may be special preparation needed. The session plan alerts the leader when advance preparation is required.

Session Format

PLANNING THE SESSION

Session Goals
Scriptural Foundation
Special Preparation

GETTING STARTED

Opening Activity
Opening Prayer

LEARNING TOGETHER

Video Study and Discussion
Book and Bible Study and Discussion

WRAPPING UP

Closing Activity
Closing Prayer

OPTIONAL ELEMENTS

Journaling

Journaling is a wonderful way to encourage more individual reflection and more extensive interaction outside the group sessions. You can promote the use of a journal by using one of your own as part of your preparation and class time. Group members can use any sort of book they would like for journaling, from a composition book to a bound, blank journal to sheets of loose-leaf paper. Some groups even use dedicated internet sites where they can post ideas and share thoughts. That approach gives you a permanent record of what you have learned and where you still have questions. Offer encouragement to those who decide to use the journal for reflecting on the reading, writing questions for future learning, and considering commitments they might take for their own spiritual growth. Some of the exercises suggested in the session plans can be done in the journal during the class session.

Connect with Proverbs in Your Church and in the Arts

Proverbs: Pathways to Wisdom was created with a four-week study in mind. Invite your group members to take full part in the life of your community of faith during these weeks. Coordinate with your church leaders to find opportunities to engage members with Proverbs in Sunday school and educational settings or even with your pastor to create broader engagement through your regular worship service or other church activities.

You may also decide to listen to songs together inspired by or in a similar spirit to the Book of Proverbs. Similarly, there may be films or television episodes that relate to themes within the proverbs, the seeking of wisdom, and pathways of life. What do the musicians and filmmakers draw from the biblical text? How does their work complement your study of Proverbs and help you engage with this book?

HELPFUL HINTS

Preparing for the Session

1. Pray. You are on an important journey. Pray for God's guidance as you discern and lead. Pray, as well, for the members of your group.

2. Before each session, familiarize yourself with the content. Read the book chapter again, and reread the proverbs upon which the chapter is based. Take your time with the Scripture reading; savor every word. If you can, read it in more than one translation.

3. Depending on the length of time you have available for group meetings, you may or may not have time to do all the activities. Select the activities in advance that will work for your group time and interests.

4. Choose the session elements you will use during the group session, including the specific discussion questions you plan to cover. Be prepared, however, to adjust the session as group members interact and as questions arise.

5. Have your own sense of how you might respond to the questions, and if you wrestle with any of them, tell your group. This may lead to fruitful discussion concerning different interpretations of the proverbs.

6. Prepare the room where the group will meet so that the space will enhance the learning process. Ideally, group members should be seated around a table or in a circle or semi-circle so that all can see one another. Movable chairs are best because the group

will sometimes be forming pairs or small groups for discussion.

7. Bring a supply of Bibles for those who forget to bring their own.

8. For most sessions you will also need a whiteboard and markers, or an easel with large sheets of paper and markers. You will also see suggestions for preparing large sheets of paper before the sessions.

Shaping the Learning Environment

- Begin and end on time.

- Create a climate of openness, encouraging group members to participate as they feel comfortable.

- Not all members of the group may know one another. Even if people do know one another, have them introduce themselves. They might share a joy or concern, they might talk about what specifically interests them about the Book of Proverbs, or they might share a favorite proverb or a question they've always had about Proverbs.

- Name tags can be helpful, even in groups where everyone is supposed to know one another.

- Remember that some people will jump right in with answers and comments, while others need time to process what is being discussed.

- If you notice that some group members seem never to be able to enter the conversation, ask them if they have thoughts to share. Give everyone a chance to talk, but keep the conversation moving. Moderate to prevent a few individuals from doing all the talking.

- Communicate the importance of group discussions and group exercises.

- If no one answers at first during discussions, do not be afraid of silence. Count silently to ten, then say

something such as, "Would anyone like to go first?"
If no one responds, venture an answer yourself and
ask for comments.

- Model openness as you share with the group. Group
  members will follow your example. If you limit your
  sharing to a surface level, others will follow suit.

- You might share some questions of your own that
  you have, which will help avoid the impression that
  you know everything (even if you do!).

- Encourage multiple answers or responses before
  moving on. You can assure group members that there
  may be more than one good answer to a question.

- To help continue a discussion and give it greater
  depth, ask, "Why?" or "Why do you believe that?" or
  "Can you say more about that?"

- Affirm others' responses with comments such as
  "Great" or "Thanks" or "Good insight," especially
  if it's the first time someone has spoken during the
  group session.

- Monitor your own contributions. If you are doing
  most of the talking, back off so that you do not train
  the group to listen rather than speak up.

- Remember that you do not have all the answers. Your
  job is to keep the discussion going and encourage
  participation.

Managing the Session

- Honor the time schedule. If a session is running
  longer than expected, get consensus from the group
  before continuing beyond the agreed-upon ending
  time.

- Involve group members in various aspects of the
  group session, such as saying prayers or reading the
  Scripture.

- Note that the session guides sometimes call for breaking into smaller groups or pairs. This gives everyone a chance to speak and participate fully. Mix up the groups; try to discourage the same people pairing up for every activity.

- As always in discussions that may involve personal sharing, confidentiality is essential. Group members should never pass along stories that have been shared in the group. Remind the group members at each session: confidentiality is crucial to the success of this study.

Meeting Online

- Meeting online is a great option for a number of situations. During a time of a public-health hazard, such as the COVID-19 pandemic, online meetings are a welcome opportunity for folks to converse while seeing one another's faces. Online meetings can also expand the "neighborhood" of possible group members, because people can log in from just about anywhere in the world. This also gives those who do not have access to transportation or who prefer not to travel at certain times of day the chance to participate.

- There are a number of platforms for online meetings. Google has two products, one called Google Hangouts and one called Google Meet. You need only a Google account to use them, and that is free.

- Another popular option is Zoom. This platform is used quite a bit by businesses. If your church has an account, this can be a good medium. Individuals can obtain free accounts, but those offer meetings of no longer than 40 minutes. For longer meetings (which you will want for this study), you must pay for an account.

- Some other platforms: GoToMeeting, Web Meeting, Microsoft Teams, and others. Search the internet for "web conferencing software," and you will probably find a link to top-ten rating sites that can help you choose.
- Training and practice
  » Choose a platform and practice using it so you are comfortable with it. Engage in a couple of practice runs with another person.
  » Set up a training meeting.
  » In advance, teach participants how to log in. Tell them that you will send them an invitation via email and that it will include a link for them to click at the time of the meeting.
  » For those who do not have internet service, let them know they may telephone into the meeting. Provide them the number and let them know that there is usually a unique phone number for each meeting.
  » During the training meeting, show them the basic tools available for them to use. They can learn others as they feel more confident. Make the meeting fun by showing some amusing content, such as the Facebook page Church Humor (www.facebook.com/ChurchLOL/).
- The real meetings
  » Early invitations. Send out invitations at least a week in advance. Many meeting platforms enable you to do this through their software.
  » Early log in. Participants should log in at least ten minutes in advance, to test their audio and their video connections.
  » Talking/not talking. Instruct participants to keep their mics muted during the meeting so that extraneous noise from their location does not

interrupt the meeting. This includes chewing or yawning sounds, which can be embarrassing!

» Signaling. When it is time for discussion, participants can unmute themselves. However, ask them to raise their hand or wave when they are ready to share, so you can call on them. Give folks a few minutes to speak up. They may not be used to conversing in web conferences.

» Show and tell. Make good use of visual media, since it is available on these platforms and audio only can get boring. Be sure to learn how to play the *Proverbs* videos available for this study, whether you choose to play segments from the DVD or streaming video. Show artwork, cartoons, drawings, and so forth, always asking permission if an item is from a participant. Make sure any background décor you want to be seen is visible. Consider placing Proverbs-related art or wall hangings in the background of the room where you are participating.

Session 1

Reading the Proverbs Wisely

PLANNING THE SESSION

Session Goals

As a result of conversations and activities connected with this session, group members should begin to

- explore how Proverbs leads us in pathways to wisdom;
- understand the importance of teachability when reading the proverbs;
- see how recognizing our own limitations is essential for finding wisdom;
- appreciate the role of wise counsel.

Scriptural Foundation

The proverbs of Solomon, son of David, king of Israel:

To know wisdom and instruction,
*   to understand words of insight,*
to receive instruction in wise dealing,
*   in righteousness, justice, and equity;*
to give prudence to the simple,
*   knowledge and discretion to the youth—*
Let the wise hear and increase in learning,
*   and the one who understands obtain guidance.*
*   (Proverbs 1:1-5)*

The way of a fool is right in his own eyes,
*   but a wise man listens to advice.*
*   (Proverbs 12:15)*

Special Preparation

- If you are not in a room with a large table, prepare the room with seating arranged in a circle so that everyone will be able to see one another.

- Have name tags available as well as pens and markers for the tags.

- Have available paper, pens, pencils, and other drawing materials.

- Also have available large sheets of paper or a whiteboard with markers for writing.

- Provide Bibles for those who may not have brought one. Encourage participants to bring a Bible for future sessions. Although the book uses biblical quotations from the ESV (English Standard Version), let participants know that they can bring whatever version they may have, for example, NRSV (New Revised Standard Version), NIV (New International Version), KJV (King James Version), and so on;

sometimes it is helpful to share different translations. You can remind them that the Old Testament is written in Hebrew, so that all translations are approximations and that the same term can be translated in different ways.

GETTING STARTED

Opening Activity

APPROACHING THE PROVERBS

As participants arrive, greet them and invite them into a circle of chairs or to the table. Especially if you are working with a newly formed group, have everyone write their name on a name tag and put it on. Begin the session with brief introductions.

Tell the group that this study will explore the Book of Proverbs. In these four sessions, we will be examining individual proverbs and the Book of Proverbs as a whole, focusing on proper approach and listening to the proverbs, as well as applying the proverbs to our lives.

Ask the group members to share, without looking in the study book or a Bible, any biblical proverbs they know, either chapter and verse quotations or paraphrases. As participants share, write their responses on a large piece of paper titled "Biblical Proverbs" posted in a visible spot in the room. After the exercise, save this paper for use in a future session.

Opening Prayer

Pray together using the following prayer or a prayer of your own choosing:

God of all wisdom, who guides us in all our path-
ways, thank you for bringing us together here. Thank
you for the Book of Proverbs and for the time we have
together to study and to share. Please open our ears
and eyes to hear your voice as we read and discuss, to
seek your wisdom in the text and in our conversation.
We ask you to lead us as we seek the way of wisdom,
and light the path we walk in its pursuit. Humble
our hearts; open our ears; open our eyes. Amen.

LEARNING TOGETHER

Video Study and Discussion

Introduce the group to Dr. Dominick S. Hernández, author of *Proverbs: Pathways to Wisdom*, and assistant professor of Old Testament Interpretation at The Southern Baptist Theological Seminary. Dr. Hernández holds a PhD in Hebrew Bible and has specific expertise in biblical wisdom literature, Old Testament, and the Jewish holidays. He has taught at a number of distinguished institutions, including Moody Bible Institute, having given courses in Near Eastern Literature, the Dead Sea Scrolls, and—particularly relevant to the Book of Proverbs—wisdom literature.

Play the first track on the *Proverbs: Pathways to Wisdom* DVD: "Session 1: Reading the Proverbs Wisely" (running time is approximately 9 minutes).

After the video session plays, invite discussion and questions from the group. To spark conversation, ask group members to consider this excerpt from the video session and the questions that follow:

> If we approach the Book of Proverbs like I
> approach puzzles, we might be a little bit over-
> whelmed. We might think that there [are]

hundreds of pieces that we sort of have to put together in order for it to make sense, when in actuality, the Book of Proverbs really does make a lot of sense if we understand it to be one work of a literary genius. You see, in the Book of Proverbs, there are also sort of these corner puzzle pieces that we can recognize—themes that start to show up over and over and over again, that we can put at the corners of our reading. And then we realize there [are] sort of these border pieces that we can put together. And then we match the colors, as it were, with proverbs that are similar in theme and similar in texture. And so, the [Book of] Proverbs, to a certain extent, is like a puzzle, but we have to approach it like a puzzle aficionado [would]—ready to put this together and enjoying the process.

- How is the Book of Proverbs like a puzzle?
- What might be some of the "corner pieces" and "border pieces" we find in Proverbs?
- What other parts of the video stood out to you?
- What did you learn about the Book of Proverbs or how to approach it that you didn't already know?

Book and Bible Study and Discussion

The Wise Hear with Their "Eyes"?

Invite two members of the group to engage in a small demonstration. Give one participant a piece of paper and a pencil or pen. They are going to draw something, but they don't know what. The other group member's job will be to give the "drawer" instructions for the drawing. Have the person doing the drawing close her or his eyes. Then whisper to the second participant something like "square," "arrow," or "happy face." That participant must then give step-by-step instructions for the drawing, which the drawer must follow exactly in order to complete the image. They *cannot* tell the drawer what they are drawing, only how to do it. This can be done more than once with simpler and more complex shapes, or the entire group can be divided up into pairs who take turns in each role. After each attempt, the drawer and the group must see if they can accurately identify the shape that was to be drawn.

"In order to read Proverbs wisely," Dr. Hernández writes, "the reader must first approach the book in the posture of one who is fully dedicated to hearing—that is, receiving and obeying instruction. It is not until one's disposition is in the correct state that the knowledge taught through the proverbs can be properly applied in one's personal pathway." And later, he says,

> In Proverbs, the wise hear with their eyes. The eyes guide the readers on their pathway to increasingly attaining more wisdom, which is one of the wise reader's ultimate goals in life. If you close your eyes, you close your ears and refuse to listen to the wisdom that the writer intends to impart. Closing one's ears is actually what is repeatedly presented as counterintuitive throughout Proverbs. If you do not hear instruction, you cannot see where you are going.

Following the activity, consider the questions below.

- What does it mean to hear with our eyes?
- How does listening in a new way challenge us to receive instruction?
- Why does Dr. Hernández ask us to listen to the text with our eyes? What manner of reading does this suggest?
- How does the author's repeated call for the reader to hear help him get across his main points?

- The Book of Proverbs tells us that it is not those who already know who are wise, but those who listen and receive instruction constantly. How does this counterintuitive call reflect your own experience? How are listening and wisdom related?

THE "PRECIOSO TESORO" OF TEACHABILITY

Invite the group to consider the following passage from *Proverbs: Pathways to Wisdom.*

> Every few minutes during any family gathering, my grandmother would turn to one of her grandchildren and say, "*La juventud es un precioso tesoro,*" or, "Youth is a precious treasure." My grandmother was determined to encourage young people to recognize the blessing of still looking forward to most of their years. . . . Proverbs uses repetition as a way of leaving a lasting impact upon the reader. The repetition we observe in Proverbs begins at the most fundamental rhetorical level in the simple recurrence of words and phrases throughout the book that serve as building blocks for communicating about key concepts (such as wisdom, knowledge, instruction).

Ask the following questions:

- What are some of the *preciosos tesoros*, or precious treasures, of your life? Which ones do you wish you had valued more than you did? How do your *preciosos tesoros* influence your interaction with younger people, especially in your family?
- How does repetition play a role in your daily thought life and spiritual life? What do you repeat to yourself? What do you repeat to others? How might you consciously engage in repetition in order to grow in wisdom and help others do the same?

- Looking back at the discussion of "corner pieces" and "border pieces" in Proverbs, how are the pieces that are beginning to emerge similar to or different from what you expected? How can repeating these "corner pieces" help us as we explore the Book of Proverbs?

THE IRONY OF READING PROVERBS

Ask a member of the group to read each of the following two passages, one from the introduction to the Book of Proverbs (1:1-5) and one from Proverbs chapter 12 (12:15). Then consider the questions that follow.

> *The proverbs of Solomon, son of David, king of Israel:*
>
> *To know wisdom and instruction,*
> *   to understand words of insight,*
> *to receive instruction in wise dealing,*
> *   in righteousness, justice, and equity;*
> *to give prudence to the simple,*
> *   knowledge and discretion to the youth—*
> *Let the wise hear and increase in learning,*
> *   and the one who understands obtain guidance.*
> *(Proverbs 1:1-5)*
>
> *The way of a fool is right in his own eyes,*
> *   but a wise man listens to advice.*
> *(Proverbs 12:15)*

- How are the words from chapter 12 an echo of the introduction?
- What is the implication from chapter 12 about how the Book of Proverbs is intended to be read?
- How do the proverbs teach us "to know wisdom and instruction, to understand words of insight"?
- In the introduction, the author of Proverbs says that the wise hear the proverbs and "increase in learning." How does this characterize wisdom? As a trait or as a process? Please explain.

- Jesus said we should not call others fools (Matthew 5:22), but the author of Proverbs has no problem doing so. What do you make of that difference?
- How can the church help prepare people to be listeners and learners who seek advice?

RECEIVING INSTRUCTION FROM OTHERS: "WHOEVER HAS EARS TO HEAR . . ."

Read aloud these proverbs:

> *An intelligent heart acquires knowledge,*
> *and the ear of the wise seeks knowledge.*
> (Proverbs 18:15)

> *By insolence comes nothing but strife,*
> *but with those who take advice is wisdom.*
> (Proverbs 13:10)

> *Apply your heart to instruction*
> *and your ear to words of knowledge.*
> (Proverbs 23:12)

- In the book, Dr. Hernández writes, "Listening is active in Proverbs. Proverbs calls upon the reader to *actively* seek out knowledge and advice." What verbs are used in these passages? How are these calls to active listening different, compared with what we often think of when we think of the Book of Proverbs?
- Proverbs 18:15 speaks of the "intelligent heart" and the "ear of the wise." What do you make of these body parts being associated with these specific traits? How does this language relate back to "listening" with our "eyes"?
- Thinking about Proverbs 13:10, what characterizes good advice? The proverbs tell us to take advice, but how can we know whose advice is worth taking?

- In Christian circles, we often speak of applying Scripture to our hearts. In Proverbs 23:12, how do we *apply our hearts* to instruction?

LIMITATIONS OF OUR KNOWLEDGE: THE SEAT BELT VS. OUR OWN STRENGTH

For this activity, you will need to prepare by cutting a Priority Mail envelope (or another such piece of the material known as Tyvek) into strips—one for each member of your group. On each strip, you can write Proverbs 28:26: "Whoever trusts in his own mind is a fool, / but he who walks in wisdom will be delivered." Alternatively, you can write just the Scripture reference or simply the word *Wisdom*.

Refer to these as strips of "paper" and hand them out to the group. Then, invite group members to try to tear their strip of "paper." They will be unable to do so as the material is specifically made to withstand tearing. Then you can reveal to them that this is not ordinary paper, but a material that is designed to withstand a great deal of wear. It's even used on the outside of houses under construction to protect them!

Relate this to the seat belt story Dr. Hernández shares in the book. Seat belts, like Tyvek, are specifically designed to be strong enough to withstand great force.

(If you're unable to conduct the above activity, simply read the seat belt story from the book and talk about the fact that seat belts are stronger than we are and are designed to keep us safe.)

At the end of the activity, reflect as a group on the following questions:

- What was it like to try to tear a piece of paper and find yourself unable to do it?
- How did testing the strength of the material in your own hands help you know it could be trusted for other purposes?

- How does this relate to trusting in the wisdom of the teachings in Proverbs?
- How is it possible to truly know something is wise?
- What is stronger? Our own strength or God's? How did you come to this conclusion?
- Is trusting in something stronger than ourselves an act of weakness or of strength? Please explain.

WALK WITH THE WISE!

Throughout this study, we have been talking about the path to wisdom as the way in which we walk. But this chapter emphasizes that how and where we walk in life is at least equaled in importance by who it is with whom we choose to walk. Walking in the way of the wise includes walking *with* the wise. As Proverbs 13:20 tells us, "Whoever walks with the wise becomes wise, / but the companion of fools will suffer harm." "In some cases," Dr. Hernández writes, "walking with the wise implies living alongside people who are further along in their journeys and can provide practical wisdom and instruction about common life experiences."

Read the story Dr. Hernández tells of Carl and Barbara; then reflect as a group on the following questions:

- How do Carl and Barbara show themselves to be wise?
- Why is it important that Carl and Barbara invite others to come alongside them?
- Dr. Hernández says everyone needs a Carl and Barbara in our lives. Whom have you looked to as guides in the way of wisdom in your life?
- How has your life been different—in ways either positive or negative—because of choices you made about whom you walk with?
- How have you strived to be one others have chosen to walk with as one who is wise?

- If you are someone others choose to walk with, how can you make it a point to continue to follow the examples of others who are wise?

WRAPPING UP

Closing Activity

WISE READING, WISE WALKING

As you reflect on this chapter, think about the following questions as a group:

- When we started, did Proverbs feel like a lot of scattered puzzle pieces? If so, are you starting to see some corners and borders now?
- What ways do you think you might apply the concept of "listening with your eyes"?
- What are some precious treasures you will focus on?
- How can actively listening to Proverbs help us walk in the way of wisdom?

Closing Prayer

If the group is using a common biblical translation, invite them to read aloud Proverbs 8:33. Alternatively, ask a member of the group to read it aloud.

> "Hear instruction and be wise,
> and do not neglect it."
>
> (Proverbs 8:33)

God who speaks, who instructs, who hears our call and teaches us to listen, aid us as we seek to find your voice. Humble us to know your strength. Comfort us to know that it is your strength that holds us. May we be wise, listen to the wise, and never neglect the way of your wisdom. Amen.

Session 2

Presenting the Pathways

PLANNING THE SESSION

Session Goals

As a result of conversations and activities connected with this session, group members should begin to

- recognize the way of Wisdom and the way of Folly;
- develop a healthy fear of the Lord;
- consider carefully the meaning of trusting in the Lord and leaning not on their own understanding;
- reflect on Wisdom in a new way.

Scriptural Foundation

Trust in the LORD with all your heart,
and do not lean on your own understanding.
In all your ways acknowledge him,
and he will make straight your paths.

(Proverbs 3:5-6)

Special Preparation

- Prepare the room with seating arranged in a circle or around a table so that everyone will be able to see one another.
- Have name tags for all returning as well as for new members.
- Have available paper, pens, pencils, and other drawing materials.
- Also have available large sheets of paper or a whiteboard with markers for writing.
- Provide Bibles for those who may not have brought one.
- If you have access to Bible dictionaries, have them available for participants to use.

GETTING STARTED

Opening Activity

PRESENTING THE PATHWAYS

You might have the group introduce themselves again. This will be helpful especially for new members. As they introduce themselves, they could share a quality they think might befit a straight or crooked path, the way of Wisdom or the way of Folly.

Make a list of these characteristics on a large sheet of paper. Set the paper aside to revisit at the end of the session.

Opening Prayer

Speak aloud the following prayer or a prayer of your own:

God of the straightened path, we seek to fear and acknowledge you in all our ways. Find us in our crookedness. Reach out to us as we wander. Call us to the path of wisdom and please make it straight for us because we stray easily—in our words, in our actions, in our focus, and in how we use our time. We devote this time we have together to you and pledge ourselves to following your way with all our hearts. Amen.

LEARNING TOGETHER

Video Study and Discussion

Play the second track on the *Proverbs: Pathways to Wisdom* DVD: "Session 2: Presenting the Pathways" (running time is approximately 8 minutes).

After the video session plays, invite discussion and questions from the group. To spark conversation, ask group members to consider this excerpt from Dr. Hernández regarding how Proverbs 3:5-6 relates to the overall study of the book:

> How is it possible to acknowledge the Lord in all of our ways? Well, that's precisely what the Book of Proverbs is teaching. It's teaching [that] when God gives a command, you say yes to that and you are obedient to that command. You are acknowledging God in every aspect of your life. Every single thing that God asks you to do or not to do, you acknowledge that, you recognize that, and you walk in that. Notice the "walk"— walking and way—imagery that we have here.

- What do you think of Dr. Hernández's statement? How is it possible to acknowledge God in every aspect of life?
- What are some areas of life in which we fail to acknowledge God, or in which we may not even think of acknowledging God?
- Why is walking imagery so important in the Book of Proverbs?
- What other parts of the video stood out to you?
- What did you learn about Proverbs 3:5-6 or other things discussed in the video that you didn't already know?

Book and Bible Study and Discussion

A Favor . . . Anyone?

In the book, Dr. Hernández discusses the aversion his students have to volunteer to do an unknown favor for him in class and relates this to our general rejection of the idea of going down the path to foolishness. Who would volunteer for that? Have a member of the group read out loud the following passage from Proverbs. Consider as a group the questions that follow.

> Hear, my son, your father's instruction,
>   and forsake not your mother's teaching,
> for they are a graceful garland for your head
>   and pendants for your neck.
> My son, if sinners entice you,
>   do not consent.
> If they say, "Come with us, let us lie in wait for blood;
>   let us ambush the innocent without reason;
> like Sheol let us swallow them alive,
>   and whole, like those who go down to the pit;
> we shall find all precious goods,

> we shall fill our houses with plunder;
> throw in your lot among us;
>   we will all have one purse"—
> my son, do not walk in the way with them;
>   hold back your foot from their paths,
> for their feet run to evil,
>   and they make haste to shed blood.
> For in vain is a net spread
>   in the sight of any bird,
> but these men lie in wait for their own blood;
>   they set an ambush for their own lives.
> Such are the ways of everyone who is greedy for
> unjust gain;
>   it takes away the life of its possessors.
>   *(Proverbs 1:8-19)*

- As Dr. Hernández notes, almost no one volunteers for something they believe to be evil or foolish. In this passage, we see a warning against following others in some fairly obviously evil deeds. In what other things might we be invited to join that might not seem so evil to us at first?

- What does this passage say about the results of greed and self-interested actions?

- The father in this passage tells the son of those who might entice him, "these men lie in wait for their own blood." What does this say about the fruits of foolishness?

- The passage states, "For in vain is a net spread / in the sight of any bird." How might we be birds to the nets others set?

- The father's instruction and the mother's teaching are described as "a graceful garland for your head / and pendants for your neck." By contrast, what might foolish teachings look like, were we to wear them?

FEARING THE LORD IS BETTER THAN FEARING SNAKES

Have two members of your group each read one of the following two passages from the book out loud or read them to the group yourself and ask the group to respond to the questions that follow.

> The fear of the Lord is a respect for God that encourages us to respond to God's word in obedience. Those who fear the Lord believe his word and faithfully live in accordance with the Lord's instruction. As his children, we fear the Lord because we trust that he desires the best for us and has given us practical instruction like Proverbs in order to walk on a God-honoring pathway toward genuine wisdom. In the case of us potentially straying from the path, the proverbs correct us and remind us of the eventual consequences of the pathways of wisdom and of wrongdoing. Through the instructions of Proverbs, we know that the Lord desires to both set us and guide us on the right pathway. Fearing the Lord is taking this truth set out in his word seriously.

> • • • • •

> To its early readers, some of Israel's proverbial collection might have paralleled common traditional wisdom that could have been attributed to the local deity that was worshipped in any given geographical area.

> That is, until the "fear of the LORD" is introduced.

> In Proverbs, the call is to recognize that the starting point of acquiring knowledge and wisdom is directly related to obeying the Lord's instruction. In contrast to other traditions that revere a "god" and believe in some sort of universally

applicable wisdom, the specific language of Proverbs relates the instruction in the book to the personal name of the covenant God of Israel—the LORD. Readers are commanded to heed the instruction and walk in the way of the one true God, making Proverbs distinct from any other wisdom that might have been circulating in the ancient Near East at that time.

- *Fear* seems to be a difficult word in these passages. How have you had to adjust your understanding of "fear of the LORD"? How may you have misunderstood the concept of the fear of the Lord?

- Dr. Hernández notes that fear of—respect for—the Lord inspires obedience. Fear of punishment (as in 1 John 4:18) can also inspire obedience. Why is one kind of obedience preferable to God over the other?

- It is also important that these passages encourage fear of "the L-O-R-D," or YHWH, instead of allowing the reader to assume or insert any deity they preferred. Why was this so significant in the ancient Near East? How is it significant today?

- How does the idea of fearing the "L-O-R-D" influence your understanding of these and other biblical passages that focus on the importance of the name of God? What names or titles for God are significant for you in your understanding of and relationship to God?

"THE WAY OF WISDOM . . ."

We have been talking about wisdom as a goal, the destination of our paths. But Proverbs goes a step further and personifies wisdom, giving voice to her call, her invitation to those who have ears to hear, but have so far refused to listen. This is not a voice without authority. "True wisdom,"

Dr. Hernández writes, "is depicted as coming through the mouth of the Lord. Thus, when Wisdom shouts out and pleads for attention, she is not being arrogant and bombastic; Wisdom is speaking in the name of the Lord."

Read the passages below aloud and discuss them using the questions that follow.

> *Wisdom cries aloud in the street,*
>   *in the markets she raises her voice;*
> *at the head of the noisy streets she cries out;*
>   *at the entrance of the city gates she speaks:*
> *"How long, O simple ones, will you love being simple?*
> *How long will scoffers delight in their scoffing*
>   *and fools hate knowledge?*
> *If you turn at my reproof,*
> *behold, I will pour out my spirit to you;*
>   *I will make my words known to you."*
>
> *(Proverbs 1:20-23)*

> *For the Lord gives wisdom;*
>   *from his mouth come knowledge and*
>   *understanding;*
> *he stores up sound wisdom for the upright;*
>   *he is a shield to those who walk in integrity,*
> *guarding the paths of justice*
>   *and watching over the way of his saints.*
>
> *(Proverbs 2:6-8)*

- Wisdom is depicted as crying aloud in the street, the markets, and "at the head of the noisy streets." Where might she be crying out today? In what settings might we look for Wisdom to be calling to us? How is it possible to know whether or not we are heeding her call?
- Wisdom seems frustrated that people are not listening to her, yet she continues to call. How might this reflect God's calling to us and to the world around us?

- What might be the relationship between Wisdom calling out in the streets and the Lord "guarding the paths of justice and watching over the way of his saints"?

". . . VERSUS THE WAY OF WRONGDOING"

Dr. Hernández discusses the way of wrongdoing from three different perspectives: "Closed to Correction—Independent from Instruction," "Dumb Decisions," and "The Messy Aftermath of Dumb Decisions." These three concepts cover themes from Proverbs regarding *why* we may follow the way of wrongdoing, *how* we follow that path, and *what* consequences follow us when we do.

Each of the three passages below represents one part of this picture. Have three different group members read one passage each or read them aloud to the group; then discuss them using the questions provided.

"Because I have called and you refused to listen,
   have stretched out my hand and no one has
   heeded,
because you have ignored all my counsel
   and would have none of my reproof,
I also will laugh at your calamity;
   I will mock when terror strikes you,
when terror strikes you like a storm
   and your calamity comes like a whirlwind,
   when distress and anguish come upon you.
Then they will call upon me, but I will not answer;
   they will seek me diligently but will not find me."
                                        (Proverbs 1:24-28)

The woman Folly is loud;
   she is seductive and knows nothing.
She sits at the door of her house;
   she takes a seat on the highest places of the
   town,

calling to those who pass by,
who are going straight on their way,
"Whoever is simple, let him turn in here!"
And to him who lacks sense she says,
"Stolen water is sweet,
and bread eaten in secret is pleasant."
But he does not know that the dead are there,
that her guests are in the depths of Sheol.
(Proverbs 9:13-18)

The iniquities of the wicked ensnare him,
and he is held fast in the cords of his sin.
He dies for lack of discipline,
and because of his great folly he is led astray.
(Proverbs 5:22-23)

- In the first passage (Proverbs 1:24-28), Lady Wisdom's frustration has finally caused her to turn away. Those who have been closed to correction are given a stern warning. What causes us to be closed to correction? What attitudes of the heart keep us from receiving reproof?

- Lady Folly (Proverbs 9:13-18) sounds like a parody of a perversion of Lady Wisdom, offering a way that seems easy and tempting, as opposed to Wisdom's correction and reproof. What actions does she call people toward? How does she address, for example, the simple? Contrast this with Lady Wisdom. How do these sets of actions lead in different directions?

- In the third passage (Proverbs 5:22-23), the wicked person is ensnared by her or his own iniquities. Recall those who "lie in wait for their own blood" in Proverbs 1:18-19. How does this recurring image of crafting one's own comeuppance reflect the consequences we see of foolish actions in our own lives? How does a "lack of discipline" lead to death?

WRAPPING UP

Closing Activity

Take out the large sheet of paper from the opening activity. Look over the words contributed by the group, and ask participants to think about their images of Wisdom and Folly, of crooked and straight paths. How closely do they mirror the ones presented in Proverbs? What would they add to the list? What would they take away? Which ones do they find most personally challenging?

Closing Prayer

Offer the following prayer or one of your own:

God of the path, our way, our path, is and must be yours. Our folly is a result of our own choices, but we can always turn to you for your grace and love, no matter how far down the crooked path we may have strayed. Forgive us, Lord, for the ways we are not receptive to your correction and help us to be straightened toward the way of Wisdom. Amen.

Session 3

Practical and Personal Pathways

PLANNING THE SESSION

Session Goals

As a result of conversations and activities connected with this session, group members should begin to

- discuss the importance of speech and using words wisely;
- reflect on anger—its usefulness and the pitfalls it poses;
- understand the role of parents in providing discipline structures for children;
- consider the ethics of work;
- explore the roles of churches and individuals in the cause of protecting the vulnerable.

Scriptural Foundation

Whoever speaks the truth gives honest evidence,
*   but a false witness utters deceit.*
There is one whose rash words are like sword thrusts,
*   but the tongue of the wise brings healing.*
Truthful lips endure forever,
*   but a lying tongue is but for a moment.*
                                        (Proverbs 12:17-19)

Pride goes before destruction,
*   and a haughty spirit before a fall.*
It is better to be of a lowly spirit with the poor
*   than to divide the spoil with the proud.*
                                        (Proverbs 16:18-19)

Do not withhold discipline from a child;
*   if you strike him with a rod, he will not die.*
If you strike him with the rod,
*   you will save his soul from Sheol.*
My son, if your heart is wise,
*   my heart too will be glad.*
My inmost being will exult
*   when your lips speak what is right.*
                                        (Proverbs 23:13-16)

Open your mouth for the mute,
*   for the rights of all who are destitute.*
Open your mouth, judge righteously,
*   defend the rights of the poor and needy.*
                                        (Proverbs 31:8-9)

Special Preparation

- Prepare the room with seating arranged in a circle or at a table so everyone will be able to see one another.
- Have available paper, pens, pencils, and other drawing materials.

- Have name tags available.
- Also have available large sheets of paper or a white-board with markers for writing.
- Provide Bibles for those who may not have brought one.

GETTING STARTED

Opening Activity

FAITH LIKE A CHILD

At the beginning of the chapter, Dr. Hernández tells the story of a friend of his who, after watching Dr. Hernández's academic presentation, said he would be more impressed if Dr. Hernández could explain the presentation to Caleb, his friend's six-year-old son. Invite group members to explain some of the concepts you have been discussing in a way a young child could understand. Feel free to come up with other examples.

- What are the proverbs?
- What is the difference between Wisdom and Folly?
- How does God speak to us through Proverbs?

Opening Prayer

Read the following prayer aloud, or use one of your own:

Loving God, God of our practicalities and our personal relationships, thank you for caring about how we live our daily lives. Help us to listen with humility, to see your Spirit at work in Proverbs, and to find the path in which you would have us walk. Amen.

LEARNING TOGETHER

Video Study and Discussion

Play the third track on the *Proverbs: Pathways to Wisdom* DVD: "Session 3: Practical and Personal Pathways" (running time is approximately 10 minutes).

After the video session plays, invite discussion and questions from the group. To spark conversation, ask group members to consider this excerpt from the video session and the questions that follow:

> In this section . . . we read a bunch of proverbs that are easily memorizable, that we sometimes pull out of the book and apply to certain situations in life. There are positives and negatives to this. The positive is that we clearly believe that the proverbs—the individual proverbs—still apply in our day and age. But when we do that, we are actually sometimes stripping the book of its literary genius.

- Think about a time in which you may have applied a proverb to a situation in your life. Which proverb was it and what is its practical application?
- How is the practice of extracting proverbs from their larger context sometimes problematic?
- What other parts of the video stood out to you?
- What did you learn about the name of God, the symbol of the rod, or other ideas discussed in the video that you didn't already know?

Book and Bible Study and Discussion

SPEECH: THE *SHAKSHUKA* ENCOUNTER

In Dr. Hernández's story of the argument he got into with an Israeli food vendor over his morning *shakshuka*, he indicates that he very unwisely ran his mouth and made a potentially dangerous conflict out of what otherwise should have been a small issue. Read his conclusion to the story, along with the concepts and their accompanying proverbs below and discuss them using the questions provided.

> I was acting in a completely irrational manner, running my mouth over a few shekels and a couple of minutes. I gladly accepted the *shakshuka* in the pan, sat down, and let the goodness of Israeli fast food proceed into my mouth instead of permitting the extreme folly of my pride and arrogance to continue emanating out of my mouth. The lunacy demonstrated by my speech had almost brought about my demise.

> The truth is that we all occasionally say things that we wish we could take back because of the anguish our speech can bring to us and to others. Given the fact that verbal communication is such a significant part of human life and interaction, we are faced with innumerable decisions on a daily basis relating to how we will use our speech. The "mouth," "lips," and the "tongue" are both symbols, or metonyms, for "speech" and frequently appear in the proverbs in order to portray how speech—or even a lack thereof—is indicative of the trajectory that one is following in life.

> *When words are many, transgression is not lacking,*
> *but whoever restrains his lips is prudent.*
> *(Proverbs 10:19)*

> *Incline your ear, and hear the words of the wise,*
> *and apply your heart to my knowledge,*
> *for it will be pleasant if you keep them within you,*
> *if all of them are ready on your lips.*
> *(Proverbs 22:17-18)*

> *For lack of wood the fire goes out,*
>   *and where there is no whisperer, quarreling*
>   *ceases.*
>   *(Proverbs 26:20)*

- Consider an occasion in which you said something you wished you could take back. Were you angry when you said it? What could you have done differently?
- How might Dr. Hernández have felt while he was eating his *shakshuka*?
- Can you recall a time when you held back from using your words unwisely? How was this possible?
- Given the importance placed on our mouths and our speech in Proverbs, what might we conclude about the power and importance of our words?
- What are some methods you use to choose your words more wisely?
- Consider these concepts and proverbs and how they might apply to your speech: "The Wise Speak (Less)" (Proverbs 10:19), "The Wise Speak (Wisdom)" (Proverbs 22:17-18).

ANGER: ON "FOOL" DISPLAY

Dr. Hernández tells another story of a couple he and his family encountered at the zoo, whose argument ended up endangering the baby they had with them in a stroller. Read his conclusion to the story, along with the concepts and their accompanying Scriptures below and discuss them using the questions provided.

> Throughout Proverbs we consistently observe that those on the way of wisdom are humble people who are slow to anger. Contrarily, fools are depicted as unable to control themselves and as repeatedly giving full expression to their

anger (14:17; 29:11). Fools wear their anger on their sleeves (12:16) and seemingly cannot abstain from perpetually quarreling (20:3). In their anger, fools are irrational to the point that they are not even reasonable enough to engage in a thoughtful conversation as Proverbs 29:9 points out, "If a wise man has an argument with a fool, / the fool only rages and laughs, and there is no quiet." Unreasonable, angry people are potentially dangerous to themselves and others, as our walk in the zoo put on "fool" display.

• • • • •

It is important to note that the author of Proverbs does not imply that we should *always* refrain from *any* type of anger. As mentioned above, and considered below, there are indeed certain wrongdoings that anger the Lord (see 6:16-19). The author of Proverbs seems to be speaking against the human tendency to become offended, angry, and, consequently, divisive and hurtful in relation to issues that tempt us to become self-seeking and egotistical (29:22). Being quick to anger over these reasons does not honor the Lord, who is portrayed as constantly yearning for restoration with humans who have deeply offended him and one another.

"The LORD, the LORD, a God merciful and gracious, slow to anger, and abounding in steadfast love and faithfulness."

(Exodus 34:6)

Pride goes before destruction,
and a haughty spirit before a fall.
It is better to be of a lowly spirit with the poor
than to divide the spoil with the proud.

(Proverbs 16:18-19)

- Why is it wise to be slow to anger? Why is wearing your anger "on your sleeve" dangerous?

- If you can't reason with someone who is overcome with anger, how can you make a positive impact with him or her?

- When has anger been something you have used for good? When has it been self-seeking and egotistical?

- If God is "constantly yearning" for restoration, what should our attitude be toward those who offend us?

- Both the wise and the Lord are described in the above passages as "slow to anger." When is anger justified? How can we express or use our anger in ways that honor God?

- Think about a time when you were hurt by someone's anger. How might you be able to learn from this situation to not hurt others when you are angry?

- Pride in ourselves and our accomplishments can be a very positive thing. What kind of pride is described in Proverbs 16:18-19? How does the full passage, rather than the usually misquoted "Pride goeth before a fall" give you a better idea of what kind of pride is being named? How is it different from humility?

THE DYNAMIC FAMILY (AND FAMILY DYNAMICS)

Family dynamics, especially discipline and parent/child relationships, can be a contentious subject. To appreciate the diversity of experiences that exist in your group, have group members describe the forms of discipline they use or that were used by their parents. You might even want to make a list to show the variety of experiences reflected in the room. Then, have group members read aloud the following passages from the book and from Proverbs and discuss them using the questions provided.

The fellowship of the family is paramount in Proverbs, because we are just like malleable children and generally tend to adopt the personal characteristics and idiosyncrasies of those who are closest to us. The parental voice that we hear in Proverbs recognizes this fact and perpetually strives to convince the "son" (that is, the reader) to walk with the parents in the way of wisdom (Proverbs 1–9). By chapter 10, the child is expected to practically demonstrate his or her understanding of the importance of journeying in life with others whose conduct honors the Lord.

> *Do not withhold discipline from a child;*
> *if you strike him with a rod, he will not die.*
> *If you strike him with the rod,*
> *you will save his soul from Sheol.*
> *My son, if your heart is wise,*
> *my heart too will be glad.*
> *My inmost being will exult*
> *when your lips speak what is right.*
> *(Proverbs 23:13-16)*

- The first passage discusses the importance of recognizing that we are easily influenced by those around us. How can we use that principle to our advantage as we seek to encourage our children in the way of wisdom?
- Dr. Hernández says that proverbs concerning the "rod" relay principles and not necessarily a clear-cut system of disciplining one's children. What relevant principles are conveyed by the references to the "rod" in your opinion?
- The second half of Proverbs 23:13-16 expresses the deep joy and satisfaction in parents' hearts when they see their child proceeding in the way of wisdom. How might parents improve their relationships with their children by communicating this feeling to them?

EARNING AN HONEST LIVING

The proverbs can contain instruction that applies to certain areas of our lives both directly and indirectly. Regarding working, employment, and financial responsibility, they do both. Consider the questions below in light of the following passage from the book and accompanying proverbs:

> While Proverbs admittedly makes no mention of drug trafficking and the potential consequences that might emerge from this type of activity, it is absolutely certain that selling drugs is a modern expression of the depiction of folly within the book. Selling illicit drugs is frequently precipitated by an apathy toward legitimate work and a desire to attain quick wealth. Furthermore, drug dealing is an ultimate form of obtaining ill-gotten financial gain by way of oppressing those who are vulnerable and in need of help. The proverbs have plenty to say about these topics.

> *Whoever works his land will have plenty of bread,*
> *but he who follows worthless pursuits will have plenty of poverty.*
> *(Proverbs 28:19)*

> *Slothfulness casts into a deep sleep,*
> *and an idle person will suffer hunger.*
> *(Proverbs 19:15)*

- The first passage asks us once again to seek, not simple directives, but deeper principles. How does this example help us think about the kind of work we do?
- How have you questioned the moral integrity of doing a certain job? What did you do about it?
- How has our view of work changed since the writing of Proverbs? What about our view of money?
- What are some "worthless pursuits" that might keep us from doing good work?

- What are the rewards of work, apart from money and food?
- How can we develop habits that keep us from sloth and fatigue?

CONCERN FOR JUSTICE

For this exercise, either select a group member to read aloud the following passage from the book or read it aloud yourself. But first, select members of the group to read the proverbs cited within the passage. Then, have each member read her or his assigned proverb aloud when it is cited in the text:

> We also observe how active the Lord is portrayed to be in protecting all of the vulnerable in Proverbs. It is the Lord who protects the poor (22:22-23), it is the Lord who actively maintains the widow's boundaries (15:25), and it is the Lord who repays those who are generous to those in need (14:21b; 19:17). Proverbs calls obedient readers to recognize that those who care for the oppressed, the needy, and the weak demonstrate the character of the Lord to fellow human beings.
>
> Fearers of the Lord treat the poor with justice as they walk on their pathway to wisdom (29:7). Furthermore, those who are in positions of power are compelled to speak out upon observing injustice being carried out among the vulnerable (31:8-9). Whether or not we are in positions of worldly authority and have tremendous wealth, it is our responsibility to share our resources with the poor, to treat the less fortunate with dignity, and to afford them all of the rights that others would have (22:9; 29:14).

Ask the group to respond to the following questions:

- Since it is the Lord who cares for all these people, why shouldn't we just sit back and let the Lord care for them?
- As you read the proverbs within the context of the above passage, how did you begin to hear a cohesive voice? What was that voice saying?
- Think of other members of society who are vulnerable. How does the principle of protecting the vulnerable call us to act toward those people? How are churches responding to that call? How can they improve?
- What can you do in your own life to protect the vulnerable?

WRAPPING UP

Closing Activity

PRACTICAL, PERSONAL REFLECTION

Invite the group to draw or write about an area that was discussed in this chapter that was particularly meaningful to them. It might be speech, anger, family, work, or justice. They can share this with the rest of the group or keep it to themselves, but invite them to keep the paper with them—in their Bibles, wallets, or another safe place—as a reminder and a catalyst for prayer and reflection.

Closing Prayer

Offer the following prayer or one of your own:

Jesus, we thank you that you are the Word spoken by the Father, that you are slow to anger, that you have made us sons and daughters of God, that you depict a kingdom where all the workers earn their full wage, and that your Spirit works in us for justice. We ask for your guidance in all these practical and personal pathways, for you have walked this way before us. Amen.

Session 4

Wisdom in Practice: Proverbs 31

PLANNING THE SESSION

Session Goals

As a result of conversations and activities connected with this session, group members should begin to

- understand the structure of the Book of Proverbs as a cohesive whole;
- appreciate the themes of the book reflected in the Proverbs 31 Warrior Woman;
- reflect on the role of wives and mothers as examples, not just to women, but to everyone;
- understand the way the principles discussed throughout Proverbs are shown to work together;
- see Proverbs as a useful guide on the way of wisdom.

Scriptural Foundation

An excellent wife who can find?
　　She is far more precious than jewels.
The heart of her husband trusts in her,
　　and he will have no lack of gain.
She does him good, and not harm,
　　all the days of her life.
She seeks wool and flax,
　　and works with willing hands.
She is like the ships of the merchant;
　　she brings her food from afar.
She rises while it is yet night
　　and provides food for her household
　　and portions for her maidens.
She considers a field and buys it;
　　with the fruit of her hands she plants a
　　vineyard.
She dresses herself with strength
　　and makes her arms strong.
She perceives that her merchandise is profitable.
　　Her lamp does not go out at night.
She puts her hands to the distaff,
　　and her hands hold the spindle.
She opens her hand to the poor
　　and reaches out her hands to the needy.
She is not afraid of snow for her household,
　　for all her household are clothed in scarlet.
She makes bed coverings for herself;
　　her clothing is fine linen and purple.
Her husband is known in the gates
　　when he sits among the elders of the land.
She makes linen garments and sells them;
　　she delivers sashes to the merchant.
Strength and dignity are her clothing,
　　and she laughs at the time to come.
She opens her mouth with wisdom,
　　and the teaching of kindness is on her tongue.
She looks well to the ways of her household

and does not eat the bread of idleness.
Her children rise up and call her blessed;
her husband also, and he praises her:
"Many women have done excellently,
but you surpass them all."
Charm is deceitful, and beauty is vain,
but a woman who fears the Lᴏʀᴅ is to be
praised.
Give her of the fruit of her hands,
and let her works praise her in the gates.

(Proverbs 31:10-31)

Special Preparation

- Prepare the room with seating arranged in a circle or at a table so that everyone will be able to see one another.
- Have available paper, pens, pencils, and other drawing materials.
- Have name tags available.
- Also have available large sheets of paper or a whiteboard with markers for writing.
- Provide Bibles for those who may not have brought one.
- Be sure to have the large paper from the first session on hand.

GETTING STARTED

Opening Activity

Pᴜᴛᴛɪɴɢ Iᴛ Tᴏɢᴇᴛʜᴇʀ

Take out the paper from the first session where you wrote down the proverbs mentioned by group members in the first session. If you are able, look them up. Are they all actually in the Bible? How many were misquoted or distorted? How do they correlate with the themes and verses that have been discussed in this series?

Now, ask group members: What has changed in your perception of the Book of Proverbs throughout this study? What do you recall from the study—either major themes or specific proverbs? Write their responses on a new sheet of paper.

Opening Prayer

Read the following prayer aloud, or use one of your own:

> *God of love, as we enter our final study of Proverbs, grant us once more the eyes to see and ears to hear the purpose you have for us on our path. Tie together the long cords that have run throughout this study. May they bind our hearts to yours as we seek the way of wisdom. Amen.*

LEARNING TOGETHER

Video Study and Discussion

Play the fourth track on the *Proverbs: Pathways to Wisdom* DVD: "Session 4: Wisdom in Practice" (running time is approximately 8 minutes).

After the video session plays, invite discussion and questions from the group. To spark conversation, ask group members to consider this excerpt from the video session and the questions that follow:

> The woman that is depicted in Proverbs 31 is
> the ultimate model of wisdom. The author of
> the Book of Proverbs was a genius. Not only was
> the author able to compile all of these proverbs

and put them together in such a way that readers thousands of years later can still learn from and apply the proverbs to their lives, the author saved this wonderful poem [for] the very end of the book and organized the proverbs in such a way that there would be foreshadowing leading up to this ultimate example, this model of wisdom.

- Is this a surprising culmination for you? Why or why not?
- In what ways do you see the themes discussed throughout Proverbs depicted in this person?
- How has exclusively framing this person as a virtuous *woman* or an excellent *wife* limited her ability to be interpreted as an example for all who seek to be wise?
- Do you think she was a real woman, or is she an ideal? If she was real, who might she have been?

Book and Bible Study and Discussion

WHO IS *THIS* WOMAN?

Read together as a group or have several people read out loud Proverbs 31:10-31. Enjoy the experience!

As you read, notice how the woman is identified and the various words of praise and honor that are attributed to her. Write these words and phrases on a large sheet of paper, but leave the middle blank. Now read the following passage aloud from the book:

> The woman who is commonly described as "virtuous," "capable," "excellent," or "noble" in Proverbs 31:10 certainly resembles each one of these adjectives. Yet, one potential modifier is frequently overlooked. The same Hebrew word that is translated to the adjectives listed above is also used dozens of times elsewhere in the Bible to indicate physical strength, force, and even

an army (for example, 2 Kings 18:7). On other occasions, the word relates some sort of moral valor (for example, Ruth 3:11). Based upon the description of this woman in Proverbs 31:10-31, it is clear that both of these nuances in meaning apply. "Warrior woman" (literally, "woman of strength") is a colorful translation that encompasses the perseverance, determination, and sacrifice it takes to live life in a way that consistently honors the Lord—especially under pressing expectations and in unfortunate circumstances. This is my translation of the Hebrew, *eshet chayil*, which I will use throughout this chapter.

Now, in large letters, write "Warrior Woman" in the center of your page. Use the following questions to discuss this as a group:

- What do you think of Dr. Hernández's personal translation of "warrior woman"? Does it seem appropriate? Please explain.
- Who are the "warrior women" in your life? What characteristics encourage you to assign these women this title?
- Who has been an exemplar of wisdom in your life?

FORESHADOWING WISDOM

There are several instances of foreshadowing the appearance of the warrior woman throughout the Book of Proverbs, including mentioning the father and mother together and using language that will be returned to in Proverbs 31. Mentioning the father and mother would have been particularly unusual in the world of the Israelite social elite. "By repeatedly mentioning the parents together," Dr. Hernández writes, "the writer of Proverbs conveys that the book's wisdom emerges from both the mother and the father."

The father of the righteous will greatly rejoice;
  he who fathers a wise son will be glad in him.
Let your father and mother be glad;
  let her who bore you rejoice.
                                        (Proverbs 23:24-25)

A wise son makes a glad father,
  but a foolish man despises his mother.
                                        (Proverbs 15:20)

- Given the prominence of men in ancient Israelite society as is depicted in the Old Testament, are you surprised that the mother is so frequently mentioned in Proverbs? Why or why not?
- How are you starting to see the "warrior woman" peeking around the corners throughout the text?

THE WARRIOR WOMAN: "WORTH FAR MORE THAN *PRECIOUS JEWELS* . . ."

Have someone read each of these three passages out loud:

An excellent wife who can find?
  She is far more precious than jewels.
                                        (Proverbs 31:10)

Blessed is the one who finds wisdom,
  and the one who gets understanding,
for the gain from her is better than gain from silver
  and her profit better than gold.
She is more precious than jewels,
  and nothing you desire can compare with her.
                                        (Proverbs 3:13-15)

Take my instruction instead of silver,
  and knowledge rather than choice gold,
for wisdom is better than jewels,
  and all that you may desire cannot compare
  with her.
                                        (Proverbs 8:10-11)

- What do you think are some types of riches that might be mentioned today as less valuable than wisdom?
- Proverbs echoes itself. How might that help it be applied to the teachable heart?
- There are more parallels in the book—phrases regarding bed coverings, wealth, and strong women. Do you find all of this compelling evidence of Dr. Hernández's argument? Please explain your thoughts.
- What other foreshadowing do you see?
- After reading the Proverbs 31:10-31 passage, how might you explain Wisdom being personified as a woman in chapter 8 and elsewhere? Could the woman be the same, ideal image of wisdom?

A PORTRAIT OF GENUINE WISDOM

Have someone read out loud the following passage from the book:

> The connections mentioned above suggest that the author of Proverbs is working toward a complex illustration. Despite the fact that all of the proverbs may not have originally come from the same source (see 10:1; 25:1; 30:1; 31:1), the author of the Book of Proverbs assembled the materials into a singular composition throughout which many of the same major wisdom-related principles are reiterated. The repetition of themes relating to how people should live on the way of wisdom eventually drives toward the exemplar of wisdom in Proverbs 31.
>
> Up to this point in our study, we have approached Proverbs as puzzle aficionados. We encountered the individual proverbs as disconnected

puzzle pieces. We then took the time to read through them, supposing that there was a "big picture" at the end. We noticed that many of the pieces of proverbs "looked alike." As we began to assemble the puzzle, we noticed, through repetition, that patterns became evident, and corner puzzle pieces (major themes) emerged. As these corner pieces surfaced, some of the more difficult proverbs began to fall into place. This entire process comes to an end in Proverbs 31, where the final puzzle pieces are organized and the big picture of Proverbs materializes. In this section, we are going to arrange a couple of the final pieces together and observe the aesthetics of this masterful poem that sketches the picture of the extraordinary warrior woman.

Dr. Hernández mentions other characteristics of the warrior woman that are found throughout the Book of Proverbs: her love of family, her hard work, her honest wages, her care of the vulnerable, her wise speech, her humility, and her lack of fear. Hopefully, the puzzle pieces with which we began have taken shape into a more complete image of wisdom.

- How has the focused structure in the Book of Proverbs surprised you?
- Why do you think we tend to view the Book of Proverbs as merely a collection of random, pithy sayings?
- How does having this "road map" and image of the warrior woman as an example of wisdom help you see your way toward and further down the path of wisdom?
- How might you now look at a pile of puzzle pieces a bit differently than before?

WRAPPING UP

Closing Activity

SINGING THE PRAISES OF WISDOM

As a group, join together in reading the entirety of Proverbs 31:10-31, in much the same manner of Dr. Hernández and his family on Friday nights. Though you won't be singing together in Hebrew, recite together in English (from the ESV or another translation to which all members have access) as though you were singing a group hymn. The text is, after all, a poem, and might have been meant to be read aloud. As you read, make the reading a praise to wisdom and to YHWH, the God of all wisdom.

Closing Prayer

God of all wisdom, who guides us in all our pathways, thank you for bringing us together here. Thank you for the Book of Proverbs and for the time we have had together to study and to share. Thank you for opening our ears and eyes to hear your voice as we have read and discussed, seeking your wisdom in the text and in our conversation. As we leave this space, we ask you to tune our ears and voices to your music and regulate our heartbeats to your rhythm, that we may be singers of your song, here and in the broader world in which we live. That world is yours, and so are we. Amen.

www.ingramcontent.com/pod-product-compliance
Lightning Source LLC
Chambersburg PA
CBHW010858090426
42737CB00020B/3415

* 9 7 8 1 5 0 1 8 9 4 3 1 2 *